J. M. Hicks

The North American Bee-Keepers' Guide

J. M. Hicks

The North American Bee-Keepers' Guide

ISBN/EAN: 9783337144661

Printed in Europe, USA, Canada, Australia, Japan

Cover: Foto ©Andreas Hilbeck / pixelio.de

More available books at **www.hansebooks.com**

THE

NORTH AMERICAN

BEE-KEEPERS' GUIDE,

By J. M. HICKS,
PRACTICAL APIARIAN,
BATTLE GROUND, TIPPECANOE CO., IND.

LAFAYETTE
BEE STEAM PRINTING HOUSE,
J. L. COX & BRO., PRINTERS.
1875.

PREFACE.

In presenting this little treatise on the Honey Bee, it is not my intention to enter into a long story about what our fore-fathers did, or how they kept bees and cut out honey by the barrel or tub ful; but what I aim at will be to give the reader something that is practical and up with the times. For be assured that the science of Apiculture has and is making fast progress, and many valuable lessons have and will be learned, about the proper management of the little honey bee; knowing as I well do that there has been many books both great and small, written on the management and culture of the honey bee. I feel somewhat timid about trying to add one more work upon the subject. Yet feeling assured that there has been and is yet, many false ideas abroad in the land, concerning the breeding and management of bees, I deem it a matter of sufficient importance to unravel at least some of the mysteries of their work, (in the hive) which is most usually so constructed in shape that the novice would scarcely ever think of looking further than at the place where the bees enter their Hive for further instruction.

I trust, therefore, that in my efforts to place this Book before a reading public, and especially the Bee keepers of North America, it will be the means of doing at least some good, having had near thirty years experience in Bee keeping.

I therefore Respectfully dedicate this little volume to all lovers of the honey bee.

J. M. HICKS,
Battle Ground,
Tippecanoe County, Ind.

INTRODUCTION

THIS Book, on Bee Culture is not designed to be so over-loaded with surplus matter or technical terms as to tax the young beginners mind, and make Bee culture an endless and a laborious study. But on the contrary I design it as a book of importance to those who have never had the opportunity of knowing by practical experience what there is in the management of the (so much neglected) Honey Bee; as well I may be able to place before those who have had many years experience in the past system of handling and raising bees by what they call *luck*, (for which I truly feel sorry.) as I am well convinced from my own experience that *luck* has nothing to do with a Correct System of Bee Culture, and only rests upon a proper knowledge of nature's laws governing the ever busy little honey bee, which has been created for man's good; but oh! how sadly neglected and let go to ruin; after which man was so blind as not to know the true cause and called it his bad luck. What would we now in this enlightened age think of a man who had a horse in a stable and otherwise would wholly neglect him? You would say at once, the man would have bad luck with his horse. Just so with his bees, he has owned perhaps for years in the old fashioned round or square box hives, which he has totally neglected until they finally died and were lost, Nature's laws not even thought of once by the man and then he lays it all to his bad luck and actually tells you that he has such poor luck with bees that he cannot raise them. Reader, how many horses do you think such treatment as this man gave his bees would raise? and how fat would his hogs and sheep be if they received such treatment as the bees do, of those who pronounce bee keeping all in luck and let them go at loose ends, with Nature's was entirely neglected.

But while we have spoken of those who have thus acted very unkindly toward the little honey bee, and finally gave up in despair, let us see well to it that we, under the new dispensation of things pertaining to the welfare and prosperity of the bee, make no mistakes and ruin our stock, which if properly cared for and attended to in the right time will pay a larger income than any other investment man can make. Here let me say it is no uncommon thing to frequently hear of Bee-keepers realizing from a few stands of bees seven to ten hundred per cent.. I also will say that my humble opinion is, the only sure road to success for the Aparian is to use a Movable frame Hive of some kind, which must be a hive up with the times, so you can handle bees with ease and pleasure. This of course will be a matter for you to decide, to some extent in your own mind, from the fact, that cost as well as the facilities for handling bees depend very much upon the construction of your hive. I have tried several different hives of the movable frames as patented heretofore, among which I am better pleased with the results of the Hicks Bee Hive than any I have as yet tried.

Reader, be you who you may, let me impress upon your mind the importance of a strict adherence to the natural laws governing the most industrious insect that God has given for the good of man. As well I desire that you study the lessons herein laid down for your practical operations, which if followed will lead you to success and save many colonies of bees, which have been heretofore lost for want of a proper system of management. Very Truly,

J. M. HICKS.

THE NORTH AMERICAN Bee Keeper's Guide.

CHAPTER I.

The Natural History and Description of the Honey Bee.

THE Honey Bee is said to have existed from the earliest dawn of creation. Be this as it may, we read in Holy writ, of Bees and Honey both being found in the carcass of a lion (Judges 14th chapter, 8 verse.) It is said that the Creator gave to Adam the privilege of naming all living creatures, both of the animal and insect kingdom, among which he must have given the name of the Honey Bee; which has been a forerunner of Civilization and was no doubt brought to this continent by the puritan fathers, which has existed ever since among us. It is said that in parts of Europe the culture of the honey bee is carried on with great profit, there are as many as nine hundred colonies to the square mile. A Colony of Bees usually contains from ten to eighty thousand and in a perfect state, consisting of three kinds; 1st the queen or female, the mother of the whole hive. She lays the eggs which hatch, both workers and drones, (the lazy fathers) of the swarm or hive.

The workers are female in their sex, though not fully developed, therefore they are the honey gatherers and wax workers as well as nurse and take care of the young bees. In a word they do all the labor in and out of the hive, as well they defend themselves from all intrusions and make war upon their enemies.

Drones are Larger than the Worker Bees

and are the male Bees of the stock or swarm; they are more clumsy, their heads and trunks are covered with a fuzz or sort of hairy coat, their wings are larger than the workers and when they fly the sound is very different from the other bees. They have no cavities on their legs, consequently cannot carry pollen, they cannot sting, having nothing of the sort to defend themselves with; they do no labor about the hive, and are only useful to meet the young queens in the swarming season, after which, the workers expel them from the hive, killing them by stinging without mercy, which is sure death and thus ends their existence.

More About the Worker Bee.

I here wish to say something further

about the worker bees nursing their young.

I have watched with great care for hours at a time, in my Observatory Hick's Bee Hive and have invariably found the young bees becoming nurses as fast as they hatched out, thereby relieving the older bees from the duties in the hive, which it seems they were pleased to have the privelege of doing, and giving place to the young bees, and from a careful as well many and repeated observations I have made I am fully pursuaded in my own mind that the young worker when first hatched out, enters from that moment upon its duties, just as the apprentice who commences to learn a trade and thus goes on up, step by step, unto perfection; from the young nurse bee to that of a wax worker and then launches out in the open air; delving into each flower of the field and forest, for the sweet nectar to carry home where peace, harmony and wisdom dwell. The worker bee is not so large as the drone, but is of a size between the drone and the queen, and are more active both in and out of the hive, rom the fact they gather all the honey and pollen, or bee bread, which is food for the young bees, which after they once enter upon the duties as honey, pollen and propolis or glue gatherers; they only live about forty or fifty days which is the average life of a worker bee.

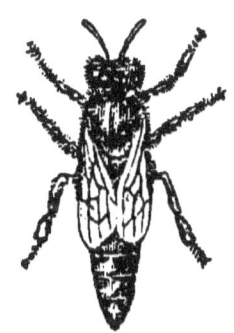

Size and Shape of Queens.

The queen is of a slender shape and much longer than the drone or worker, and as I before stated she lays all the eggs which hatch the bees, she is usually of a brighter color than the worker or drone, her wings appear to be shorter than the worker bee's wings, but this is owing to the fact her body is much longer and the wings do not cover her so completely as the wings do the other bees, she always seems to be busy moving about on the combs except when in the act of laying eggs, which she is capable of performing at the rate of two to three thousand per day.

Age of Queens not Certain.

Although it is equally true that a queen will live in many instances to be four or five years old and perform all the functions of the mother of a colony; but if the workers discover that she is about to become barren, they will at once make preparation to supercede her, and rear another Queen, in due time. Reader, I could go on and write page upon page, in connection with this subject of the honey bee, but as I promised in the outset, it was not my intention to over-load your minds with surplus matter, I will therefore in conclusion say to you, go to your hives and there learn lessons of wisdom and harmony which dwell therein, and has from the earliest dawn of creation.

A Test of Queens Laying Eggs.

In my recent observations in my observatory hive I timed a fine italian queen while in the act of laying, and she laid seven eggs per minute, which was at the rate of four hundred and twenty per hour, this of course she could not perform very long at a time, but I am well satisfied that a good prolific and healthy queen can lay at least three thousand eggs in twenty-four hours, in the proper season of the year, if the nurse or worker bees perform their duty in waiting on her by feeding and keeping up her strength and vigor which is a duty they seem to perform with great pleasure and promptness while she is in the act of laying.

Do Queens Sting.

She also has a sting which she uses only in dispatching other rival queens; and it is said often killing the young embryo queens in their cells which I doubt.

It seems to be a trait of character in queen bees. to never use their sting except on a rival queeen, at least if so I have never known or heard of an instance yet, as they only seem to have an antipathy for other queens, and have been known to meet each other in mortal combat. It usually takes about fifteen to sixteen days to hatch out a fully developed queen in a good strong colony of bees and about twenty-one days to hatch a worker bee from the egg, the drones require about twenty-four days to become fully developed and hatch out, the above time as specified depends very much upon the condition of the colony of bees, which if strong will often shorten the time a few days especially the royal queens which I have known to hatch out in twelve days from the time the workers commence the

Construction of Royal Cells.

Queen Cells are cells which resemble a peanut so much on the side of the combs and is usually constructed so as to hang nearly perpendicular, (they are much larger than any of the other cells in the comb) which causes the queen to be developed with her head downward, and allow the organs of reproduction to be fully developed, the queen cell is sometimes built around the egg, and at other times the egg is carried by the workers and placed in the cell and royal jelly is also placed in the cell with the egg, which helps with that of the cell to change its nature from that of a worker to that of a royal queen, her royalty passes about three days in the egg, five days a grub or larvæ, during which time the workers deposit so much royal food in the cell that the larvæ fairly floats in the jelly-like mass, the cell is then closed by the workers, and the larva commences to spin its cocoon which occupies about twenty-four hours, the tenth eleventh and twelfth days it remains in complete repose; then it is that transformation takes place, in which four days are passed, and generally on the sixteenth day the perfect state of the queen is attained. When she first emerges from the cell she seeks her own food like any other bee. No very particular attention is paid to her until after her impregnation; but as soon as that has taken place she is at once recognized and constantly attended by the worker bees. But her attendants are not any special or certain bees set apart for that purpose, as is often stated by some writers, but wherever the queen moves among the bees they seem to detail themselves in sufficient numbers for the purpose of feeding and caressing her in all her labors—especially so while she is in the act of laying eggs in the cells.

Impregnation of the Queen.

After hatched, it usually takes place about the fifth day after she is hatched out of the royal cell, but in some instances I have known them to go longer; yet it is very seldom, and if she should go unimpregnated until she is twenty days old you may set it down as a fixed rule that she will never have copulation with a drone; at least I have never known of an instance of the kind taking place, and have never heard of but one case that a queen has become fertilized after she was twenty days old. She usually comes out of the hive between the hours of 12 and 4 o'clock in the after-noon when the drones are flying most abundently. As before remarked, the queen usually comes out to meet the drone in the air, on the wing in order to copulate, which it is said, once performed is sufficient for life. But my experience this year 1870. has taught me that it does not always take place in the open air.

Artificial Fertilization in Confinement.

I have made three efforts this season in my Hicks Bee Hive and twice out of the three efforts I succeeded in having two beautiful Italian queens fertilized by a selected and pure drone as could be found in the City of Indianapolis.

Here I will give my plan, practiced or tried in the above cases referred to.

In the first place I procured a fruit cover which is made of a cambered or oval top shape of wire cloth; to this I made a close fiting botom of a thin piece of board and placed a piece of honey with my queen and drone, also a single worker bee in the cage and then I set my cage in the top of the Hicks Bee Hive and after I had let them remain a few hours all closed up by themselves (except the workers were allowed to come up and remain on and around the cage which kept the necessary heat.) I then examined them twice before I found any perceptible change after which I took the queen and removed her to the hive. I desired to test her qualities as to purity which I found to be all I could ask or desire her to be. Let me say the drone was dead as a door nail, in both cases above referred to. And to-day (November 1st, 1870,) I have as pretty marked italian bees as there is in the state from those queens thus fertilized.

Yet I would not say that the above plan will in every instance succeed.

See illustrated Bee Journal, of 1870, page 473, also same book page 479.

But when the queen is permitted to go at will and pleasure as in the old way to seek her own company, my opinion is that copulation takes place on the wing after which she commences laying in about four or five days.

How a Fertile Queen is Known.

A Fertile queen is known by her depositing her eggs in the cells close together in circles, each surrounding the first, and on both sides of the comb alike, sealed worker brood, will present a regular smooth surface of a brownish color.

How a Virgin Queen or Drone laying Queen is Known.

If you have an unfertile queen, she may be known by an irregular brood, a number of raised oval cells in worker combs, which shows the presence of drone brood and indicates a drone laying queen only, or a queen that is approaching barrenness, which is sometimes the case, when they become quite old, which, if the latter, will often cause the old queen to be superceded by a young queen, reared by the workers to take her place.

An Instance of Two Queens in One Hive.

I have known one instance of this kind in the summer of 1870, in a strong and full colony of Italian bees, owned by a Mr. Cal. Elliott, of the city of Indianapolis. The fertile queen can lay both kinds of eggs, that of drones and workers. This, to many, will seem quite strange; it is nevertheless true.

The Impregnating, or Seminal Fluid,

received by the queen from the drone is contained in a sac called the sperm reservoir, or spermatheca, which communicates with the ovaduct, through which the eggs pass to be deposited in the cells. Therefore, when the eggs leave the ovaries, or egg-bag, they are unimpregnated; but, in passing through the oviduct, all eggs that produce workers, or queens, are brought in contact with the mouth of the sac containing the seminal fluid, and receives a portion of it, which impregnates them, while all the eggs that hatches drones (which is the male bee) passes, it is said, through the oviduct without coming in contact with the seminal fluid. My own convictions are that the queen being fertilized it is fully carried through her system and in her blood for life, which impregnates or fertilizes the drone eggs sufficient without receiving the fluid direct from the sperm reservoir. If this is not the case, why has nature given her the instinct to know just when her eggs for workers are exhausted and go in search of drone cells, while the unfertile queen will lay her eggs in any and all cells?

It is supposed that the queen has a different motion in laying eggs in worker cells to that in drone cells, which may be true; but, so far as my experience goes, *I am firmly of the opinion that this difference comes from natural instinct, which she fully understands from her own feelings while in the act of laying, as I have sat and watched her in all the motions she made for hours at a time in my Observatory Hicks Bee-Hive, prepared expressly for the purpose,* in which I have timed her while in the act of laying, which result was as follows: The first two minutes she laid ten eggs—five each minute—and the third minute she laid seven, which made seventeen in three minutes, at which rate she would fill three hundred and forty (340) cells in an hour, and which would be eight thousand one hundred and sixty (8,160) in twenty-four hours. But it is certain that she must have some time to rest, which we must allow. This being the fact, we can safely say that a healthy and vigorous queen will lay from one thousand to three thousand eggs every twenty-four hours in the working season if honey and pollen is plentiful, all things being equal.

CHAPTER II.

On Swarming, and Why Bees Swarm.

It is an admitted fact that bees have been kept for ages past, and yet there are but few of to-day who keep bees but what are ignorant of the nature of swarming.

I shall therefore try in this connection to show briefly why stocks throw off swarms, and speak of the general characteristics of swarming.

First Swarm.

When a hive becomes full of comb, bee-bread and brood, the queen has no longer sufficient room to deposit her eggs, and the workers require more room to store their honey; preparation is therefore made for swarming. This is done by the workers, who instinctively commence the rearing of young queens. For here let me say if young queens are not reared no swarming need be looked for, neither will it take place, though they may be ever so much crowded for room. Hence it is not altogether true that bees swarm for want of room. No stock will ever cast a swarm unless the queen will leave, and she will not leave unless rival queens are being reared. It is also equally true that the old queen is the one that leads the first swarm. She, finding the cells all filled and occupied, and the rearing of young ones commenced, becomes very much agitated and each day more restless, and not being permitted by the guards and sentinels around the queen-cells to destroy them, runs rapidly over the combs, sometimes stopping upon the side of a comb and dropping her eggs among the workers, who greedily devour them. The workers also partake of the excitement. A few at first, the number gradually increasing, running rapidly over the combs, striking their attenæ at each other. And as soon as one or more of the queen-cells are capped over, the excitement still increasing among the bees, as if by pre-concert they rush to the honey cells and fill themselves with their precious stores. After each bee has partaken to their fill, the weather permitting, they rush from the hive in a perfect cloud, as if the very halls of pandemonium had been let loose among them,

The Old Queen Going With Them.

Most usually she leaves the hive when about two-thirds of the swarm are out. I have often noticed her go back two or three times, as if she wished to see if all things were in readiness before she would make the effort to fly. There are but few drones to go with the first swarm, from the fact that the old queen is impregnated for life. Hence they are not required. Instinctively they remain with the parent hive, where the young queens are being reared.

When the First Swarm is Cast

the parent hive is left without a queen, but there are several being fast developed. As before remaked, one or more of the queen-cells are generally sealed over before the old queen leaves. In about eight or nine days after the first swarm has issued a second swarm may be expected—that is, if the stock intends to cast a second swarm.

The Piping of the Queens

is often heard on the evening before the second swarm issues. This piping noise is somewhat in sound like that of a young chicken when it is making the effort to leave the shell in hatching. Suppose a first swarm had issued on Monday, just a week from the evening of the next day, which would be Tuesday evening, if you will go to the hives you will hear the cry of war, as it is so called by most of bee keepers, and is a sure token of a swarm to come off on the following day, which would be Wednesday. Yet this is not always a certain rule, for I tell you, reader, the weather has a great deal to do in bee swarming. For instance: if it has been a long, dry spell you need not be surprised at your bees if they fail to swarm at all; but let there come a good shower of rain and my word for it you will see the swarms more certain the next day, if it is a beautiful day, than if it had remained dry and parched, or sultry.

Now, one thing more I wish to call your attention to, and that is the fact of so many bee keepers claiming that as soon as a young queen is hatched she goes in search of other queen-cells, that she may tear them open and dispatch the more young and tender sister queens in their embryo state before they have time to hatch and become her rivals. Now, I wish to be plainly understood that I do not believe any such doctrine, having watched with a careful eye this very much mistaken idea, and have in many instances found that as soon as a young queen had hatched out and was of a strong and vigorous form, which is always determined and decided by the worker bees themselves, they at once proceed to gnaw open and demolish all the other queen-cells that are unhatched.

This has been a lesson of great interest to me, and feeling unsatisfied with the explanations by other bee men as to how they were disposed of, I fully prepared myself with an Observatory Hicks Bee Hive and watched with care, and in every instance the result has been as above stated. Yet, dear reader, it may be that

Queens Do Often Meet in Mortal Combat,

and *engage in a death struggle, I do not deny; but never until one or both have become fertilized. Then it is that a disposition seems to take hold and predominate for the supremacy as mistress and mother of the future colony. Again, how often is it that we are asked, Can you tell me why it is that a swarm of my bees came off with two, three or even four queens? *Yes, dear reader:* this goes to prove my theory. As above referred to, you will recollect that I have before stated that there were **guards** whose duty it was to keep watch over the queen-cells, each one having a separate set; and as fast as those queens were hatched out their guards or attendants still kept watch over their queen, preventing any others from harming her, until there might be, perhaps, two, three or even four queens hatched; and finally some one of the number, getting indignant at some of her sister queens' presence, starts out in disgust, with the sound of swarming in her shrieks, and they all go together in one common swarm, as it were, and while on the wing it is possible that one of the three or more queens may copulate with a drone, after which they settle all together, and the bee-keeper, feeling himself at a loss as to what course to pursue, concludes to have one extra large swarm of them, and actually puts them all in a flour or salt barrel, and thinks he has done all things well. So the next morning he goes out and looks about and finds two or three queens dead. Now, Mr. C., this is just the fruits of one or more of your queens having copulated with a drone while in the swarming *melee*, after which, if they would ever fight at all, it will then take place, soon after they have been hived together.. And the result is you find so many dead ones about your barrel of bees that you hived the day before.

CHAPTER III.

What a Queen-Cell Looks Like.

Having been often asked what a queen-cell looked like, I will proceed to describe, in as clear and plain manner as possible. They are usually built on the edge or side of the brood-combs, and look very much like a pea-nut. They are about three-eighths of an inch in diameter at the base, and extend downwards, gradually tapering to about half the size at the lower end or point, and is usually about one and an eighth of an inch long. It is also my humble opinion that queen cells are made of an entirely different material to that of any of the combs. And, this being the case, it is also my conviction that it is the different material which produces such a radical change in the egg, or larvæ, which makes a queen. I am well aware that many who have been bee-keepers for years differ with me on this subject. But here let me say I have been a student for the purpose of learning the mysteries of the bee hive, which has been done only by dint of study and close observation, and feel sure that what I have stated with regard to the change above spoken of, is correct. Especially so when we all admit the theory that all eggs are female in their sex except those producing drones. And any egg which a fertile queen deposits in a worker-cell will also produce a queen if transferred from said cell into a royal cell before it gets seven days old. Now, the mere change from the brood or worker-cells to that of the royal cell does not make a queen bee. But it is also necessary that the wants of the whole colony demand a queen should be raised, so that all may work in unison and harmony together, the older bees performing the labor of carrying honey, water and pollen, all of which is essential to the rearing of worker, or queen bees.

What a Royal Queen Cell is Made of.

This cell question has been for many years a puzzler to a great many bee men, and seems to be hard for most of them to understand; but I think if we apply the right means in the right way it will not be hard to determine and come at facts. Having made several tests and experiments, I now feel sure that I make a correct statement when I assert that the queen cell is made from what is known as farina, or dust of flowers, and better known as bee-bread, a large share or quantity of which, as well as that of pulp, is also used in preparing and building those royal cells, which have already been described as the cells in which the queen is raised and hatched. This forms an entirely different substance from that of any of the other cells in the hive, and which, when filled with the creamy-like food which the worker bees always supply for the queen while in a larvæ state. It has the property in it of extracting a substance from the body of the cell, which also changes its chemical nature. This, in my humble opinion, is all necessary in order to bring about the result of maturing a fully devoloped female or queen, so that when she has mated with a drone that is fully and properly organized, she is then a proper bee to lay all the eggs for replenishing the hive with worker bees and drones for future prosperity. We have examined, time and again, those cells under a microscope, and invariably found them composed of a large portion of farina, and a sufficient amount of pulp to give the cell solidity and a glossy inside coating.

Do Bees Supercede Their Queens?

To this question allow me to say they do, and often kill them in the spring of the year, after they have wintered safely through, as I have often observed. And I would further say for the benefit of all who may be interested in the little honey-bee, that this killing of queens so early in the spring of the year is one of the many causes why we lose so many stocks, and wonder to ourselves why our bees died in April, or even as late as May, after they had begun to gather bee bread and honey. The question often arises why they kill their mother and only hope of existence. To this there might be many and various answers, some of which I will give. The first is, that as soon as your, as well as your neighbor's, bees begin to fly out and go in search of food, they find it quite scarce, which frequently starts them to robbing: and in this they always kill the queen as soon as possible. When accomplished, success is theirs, and they then go with the robbers, and carry off their own honey, if they have any, to the successful hives of the robbers. Another reason is, it frequently happens that in handling your bees you get your hand on the queen, and get her scented from your hand, and in this way she is often attacked and killed as soon as you close up your hive. I have often been asked by persons visiting my apiary to let them see a queen, asserting at the same time that they have never seen a queen, which is all right; but if they knew how dangerous it was to the welfare and prosperity of the stock of bees, I feel certain they would not insist on me to show the queen, and in all probability in doing so I would lose a full stock in a short time.

CHAPTER IV.

Further Explanation of Sex.

I here wish to explain further about the sex of the eggs being determined at the time of laying; for instance, it is admitted by all Bee-keepers who lay any claim to apiarian science, that a virgin queen at twenty-one days old will lay eggs which will produce drones only: (But I say they are imperfect drones, not having the male organization fully developed, and cannot perform the functions of the male in fertilizing queens.) Hence, it must follow that the general rule holds good in the insect creation, as in the animal; for if we have a pure, imported Italian queen, which was fertilized in her mother country, where there are no other bees except the pure

Italian, and we raise pure virgin queens from her, and have no other drones, but the Black in our apiary, we now have those young queens copulate with the Black drones, and the result is a cross breed, which will be the same of all the bees and drones that said queens may raise, no matter how long she lives or how many times she is permitted to swarm, or artificially divided. Now comes the pretty part; suppose you raise the next season all your drones from this same queen that has met the black drone and queens from your imported queen again, and they copulate with the drones last mentioned; I ask, what will be the result? Answer—They will be three-quarter bloods of Italian stock, notwithstanding the opinion of Mr. S. D. Barber to the contrary, for he says the drones from such queens as are fertilized by a black drone, will be pure Italian. (See his Bee book, page 36.) I should very much hate to be compelled to have stock from such a man's apiary, who would teach such false doctrine and at the same time do so much advertising as he does. Brother Barber, I hope you will get new light, and sell better stock than I saw a few days since from your apiary, February, 1874. Now, the fact is, that the blood of such queens is tainted for life, no matter how pure they may be in their virgin state, or before they copulate with his black drone. It will also be right the reverse if we have a black queen fertilized by an Italian drone; all of her stock will be half-breeds of the two kinds, and her drones will be half-breeds also. But Mr. Barber says, by his theory, they, the drones, are pure black, or of the native bee. The same rule will hold good, as we have often seen, in the human family as well as in the animal creation: also in the swine we see the same result's of Nature's law.

But we will now leave you, dear reader, to study into cause and effect, and solve such problems for yourself. Having given you the true results of such a course of breeding, let me say, try and be honest in all your sales of Hives, Rights and Queens.

CHAPTER V.

PRACTICAL LESSON

On Transferring Bees and Brood into Movable Frame Hives.

First, get you a good roll of cotton rags, and wrap some fine wire around it, then set fire to one end, but don't let it blaze; now step boldly up to the hive of bees you desire to transfer, and blow some smoke in at the entrance until you hear the bees set up a humming noise. Now pick up your hive, bees and all, and take them to a room, or some other place where the other bees will not bother you in trying to rob. Of course you will now have your new hive in readiness, with the frames laid near by. Now give your bees a little more smoke, and in ten minutes you can lay the mouth or lower end of your old hive close to your new movable frame hive, and with a good hammer, or hatchet, and cold-chisel, cut the nails of your old hive, and take off one side. Now have a table, or bench, on which to lay your combs of brood, and procure a long-bladed knife, well sharpened on a regular scythe stone, which makes the best edge for cutting out the combs. Be careful to take out all the combs, a sheet at a time, and with a goose-feather, or small broom, brush off the adhering bees into your new hive; also, be careful and do not bruise or mar the brood in handling, and lay into a neat pile as you take it out, and brush off the bees into your new hive; after which you can take a frame and fit a comb of brood, being careful to keep the same end to the top of your frame as it stood in the old hive, and with a No. 9 or 10 bradawl make a few holes through the frame and put in wooden pins, or white thorns, which you must prepare, or get quite a number beforehand, of some tough, good wood; hickory will be best. The pins must be about two and a quarter inches long, gradually tapered like a darning needle. After you have thus fitted all the brood in the frames, place them in proper shape as they were before, with the combs near the middle of the hive. Your bees being already clustered in the hive, you will have no trouble in handling them further, only to be careful not to mash or crush them as you close up your hive gently. Now take and set the new hive where the bees formerly stood, and you will have the gratification of seeing them at work in less than thirty minutes. In a day or two go to the hive and open slowly and gently, and make a careful examination of the combs, to see that they are all in the frames properly, and that all is right; but if any have warped, straighten them, and draw out all the wooden pins that can be spared, as the combs will in two or three days be all fastened by the bees in the frames.

The above is one of the best plans, and by far the most speedy.

Why is it that Bees of the Present Day do not Swarm so Much, nor Make as Much Honey, as They Did Years Ago, During the Early Settlement of the Country?

Now, reader, you have no doubt asked this question more times than I know anything about, and in all probability have during the fairs where I have been lecturing asked me the same. And while I now attempt to give you a fair and an honest answer, let me say, it is of the utmost importance for the success of an apiary, that it should be located in a neighborhood where the bees can readily find an abundant supply of good pasturage. The success of bee-keeping depends greatly upon this. As well might a stock-grower expect to make his cattle profitable without supplying them properly with food, as to suppose that bees will live, thrive and be of benefit to their owners without obtaining constant supplies of pollen and honey, in some way, from spring to fall, with but little, if any, intermission. I suppose that any school girl or boy ten years old could very easily answer the question, if I were to ask why it is that cattle, horses and hogs that run at large now-a-days, do not thrive as well as they once did when this country was new; yet the first question has been a puzzler to many older heads than mine, and would-be *wise bee-keepers*. But they never think once that it is just as essential in the one case as in the other that the efforts of man must be put forth in furnishing the necessary supply that nature once furnished, but now shorn from the land; and if not produced through and by the effort of the bee-keeper, they will fall far short of that most bountiful and richest of all dainties, which cannot be procured in any other way than through and by the honey-bee; which was gathered from the flowers *all over this broad land of the North American Continent.* The country, in its wild state, produced in the greatest abundance an unvarying succession of flowers, from early spring until frost came, yielding for the harvesters (the Bees) unlimited supplies of beebread and honey, as well as propolis, or glue, for their use in stopping up cracks and lining their old-fashioned hives, so rudely made and furnished to them; all of which (except the old-fashioned hive) are just as essential now, as in the days of the primitive fathers, to propagate very rapidly, and to store up immense quantities of honey, bidding defiance to the moth, unless, as it sometimes happened, a disorganized colony would fall a prey to their depredations. As the forests were felled, and the country cleared and brought into a state of cultivation, this source of pasturage was in many places almost entirely cut off, until their sole dependence was on the clover and buckwheat, which lasts but about two months of the year; during the remainder of the season they cannot gather sufficient honey to supply their immediate wants. In such cases men have provided pasture and made suitable provision for all other kinds of stock, but neglected *in toto* the most faithful and productive of all servants, the Honey-Bee, which is left to provide for itself; the inevitable result of which will be their total extinction in old settled countries, unless a change is made in this direction, and pasturage supplied for them, which can be done at less expense than for any other stock, and with greater returns of profit.

I have tried in a former lesson given upon pasturage for bees, to tell you what kinds, or at least the most of the many which are valuable plants, and will now say if you who desire to keep the little pets will but half way perform your duty toward them, at the right time and in the right way, they will pay you over ten hundred per cent; besides, you will reap a rich reward from the crops thus cultivated as food for cattle, sheep, horses and hogs.* Besides, I feel quite sure you will never regret having bought this little book.

Do Queens Have a Sting? And if so, Do They Ever Use Them, and What On?

In this lesson, dear reader, let me say that Queens have stings, and use them only on rival Queens and Drones. This may seem rather strange to many who have read our lesson upon her royal dignity when we said that they never used their stings on anything except a rival Queen. But at the time we wrote that lesson we did not know quite as much as we do now about Bees or Queens. You must recollect, likewise,

---

*Alsike clover makes the best of hay, and is first-class hog pasture, which is fully substantiated by some of the first and best farmers in this neighborhood.
T. HEAD, JR.,
Battle Ground, Tippecanoe Co., Ind.

that we desire that you may fully understand that all the mysteries are not learned in a short time about bees and their habits. And let us further say that we had never known in all our experiments up to July, 1874, that a virgin Queen would wilfully, and apparently maliciously, attack an innocent drone and send him to his long home by stinging him to death without mercy. But such is the fact, and we have two living witnesses who will attest it, having seen the same incident, which we shall now relate.

We think it was about the 10th of July, 1874, that we received a letter from a Mr. D. T. Musselman, of Camden, Carroll County, Indiana, who desired us to come to his place and assist him in the artificial swarming of his Italian bees, all of which were in good condition in the Hicks Bee-Hive. We arrived at his place of residence on the 18th. He and ourself, in company with a friend, proceeded to extract honey from the combs of a few frames, and to make up some five or six extra stocks. Then he took us to a strong and vigorous hive of bees, in which he had several Italian Queens hatched, in small cages. We took one of the cages out, and as the drones were flying out on their usual excursion trips, we caught one very large and vigorous one in less than a quarter of a minute. We then thought we would try another one, which we soon caught and placed in with her royal highness, and she treated him the same way, all of which was accomplished in less than a minute's time; and strange to say, yet too true, when she thrust her sting into them, it killed them so dead that they showed no signs of life, and seemed to be perfectly hard. The queen seemed to be in a perfect rage and restless, wishing to escape from her confinement no doubt. But we will here say again, that as yet we have never known an instance where a queen has ever stung a human being or an animal of any kind.

[*See lesson on Drones.*]

More Persons than do, Should Keep Bees.

We will in this lesson try to show that

it would be well for all parties concerned, and far better for the whole country, if more people would engage in this laudable and most profitable business. In the first place, we all acknowledge that the Honey-Bee is a perfect model of industry, and shows to mankind that lazy loungers are not long tolerated in their household, but are soon expelled with a death-warrant. Again, if we would profit by wisdom's ways, we should at least have a few stands of bees in our gardens or door-yards, in order to see them occasionally, and learn industrious habits, as they are at work from early morn till dewy eve, and yield a rich return to their keeper, which cannot be procured in any other way than by the industry of the little Honey-Bee.

Again, how many there are who now are dragging out a miserable existence, who have been brought up in idleness in the homes of perhaps rich parents, and afterward become poor by not knowing how to work or economize? We would add, that if our young and rising generation would copy more after the habits of the little Honey-Bee, our prisons and poor-houses would have fewer inmates, our courts would be bothered less with cases of persons charged with criminal offences, and our State and county debts be materially reduced. In this way they would contribute greatly to their own happiness, and become good citizens and ornaments of society. Then let us in our efforts call on one and all who can control, either by purchase or lease, a few rods of Mother Earth, to get and keep a few stands of bees. Persons who live in cities, as well as those in villages and on the farm, may keep bees, and scarcely miss the time it takes to keep them in good trim, which can always be done early of a morning, the best time to perform any needed operation with your bees, such as artificial swarming, or taking a few boxes of honey, which makes a dish beautiful when properly arranged on the table at meal-time. It is by far much easier and cheaper when thus procured, than to have it to buy in the market places, especially so when honey is steadily year by year advancing in price.

We have written more on this subject

than we had at first intended, but when we see and feel the importance of it, which ought to interest every lady and gentleman, both young and old, we hardly know how and where to close our remarks, without giving you some advice as to what is best for the poor and broken-down merchant and mechanic, as well as many farmers, who have failed in business, and women who have lost their husbands and left in many cases with a house full of little helpless children to support. We say to all such, let us entreat you to try your hand at keeping a few stands of bees, as you know not what you can do until you have made the effort. We will cheerfully give you all the instructions we can, if you write to us, inclosing a postage stamp to send you an answer to your questions.

Artificially Swarming Bees.

This is one of the simplest things in bee-keeping. But before I go further into the explanation of making your new swarms, dear reader, let me say, get you a good movable frame hive, one in which you feel assured you can handle bees with ease and profit; and after you have thus made your selection, have *all* your *hives* made of the same size and pattern, having them all painted at least two or three weeks before you need them for use. This being done, you are ready for making your increase of stock, provided they are strong in numbers and plenty of brood. Now you can open one of your new hives and take out six of the frames; then open a hive of bees and take out two full frames, bees, brood and honey, all together, and replace in their stead two empty frames. Let a full frame stand between the empty ones, and put the full frames you have just taken out of the full hive into the empty hive, setting them side by side. Then operate on two more hives the same way, being careful that you do not take a queen from any one of your full stocks. This relieves them from swarming, and gives you six full frames in your new hive, which you can now place in or at the old standpoint of some strong and populous colony, by setting the old stock at the same new location and place your new hive in its stead; my word for it, they will raise a queen in a few days for themselves, as they have plenty of eggs and young brood from which to fully mature and protect themselves for at least from two weeks to fifteen days, at which time you can exchange a frame or two of brood from some populous stock, so as to prevent your new hive from swarming when the young queen comes out to meet the drone. Be careful to brush off all adhering bees of the last mentioned frames into their own respective hives, which will prevent your young queen from getting killed by the young bees, if you should make a mistake and put bees and all in together.

A Fertile Worker—How Known.

My dear reader, this is one of the many difficulties that the apiarian has to contend with in bee-keeping, and should be better understood, even by the older beekeepers. The Fertile (worker) is known only by the uneveness of the brood she produces (like that of a virgin queen), all drones and no worker bees, which will soon annihilate the whole colony—as I have before told you that drones were not self-sustaining, from the fact that they do not carry honey, bee-bread or water, as workers do. It is also true that such drones are not fully developed males; hence they are of no value in fertilizing queens. The cause of the Fertile worker being brought into existence is the fact that it was an egg, or quite a young grub, that was raised in a worker cell, in close proximity to a royal or queen cell, that has had plenty of royal cream, or food prepared and placed so near the young worker that it has been affected by the royal food intended for the young queen; but it not having a proper cell in which to become fully developed, it does not arrive at that degree of perfection in its organs of reproduction, or ovaries, as to become fertilized and lay eggs to raise bees as a fertile queen does, but being what I call a neuter. It has none of the natural fitness of nature, that is actually necessary to reproduce its species, and keep up a full family or colony of bees.

How to Get Rid of the Fertile Worker.

The way for the apiarian to get rid of them, is to exchange a few frames of brood with a good stock of bees that has plenty of eggs and young bees from a prolific queen; and my word for it, they will soon clear her out of the hive, and raise another queen for themselves.

CHAPTER VI.

On the Drone Question, and What the Drone is for.

Permit me to state first, that a full and perfect swarm of bees consists of three kinds, first, the queen, or mother of the whole colony; second, the worker, or honey-gatherer; third, the drone, the subject of which we now propose to treat. This is the male bee, and is always present in the swarming season; without which the honey-bee would soon become extinct, as it is essential from the creation up to the present time, that all created beings in all nature have two parents, a mother and a father; hence, the drone is the father of all the bees that may be raised in a regular swarm. He is only useful in fertilizing the queen, which, when once performed, puts an end to his life, and leaves the queen fertile for life. She lays all the eggs from that time on to produce both bees and drones for future swarms, without ever meeting or copulating again with another drone. This may seem like strange doctrine, but nevertheless it is true; and further let me state right here, that the queen can and does lay frequently as high as 3,000 eggs in a day and night, in the height of the honey harvest; and will in any reasonable honey season lay on an average 1,500 in twenty-four hours. This no doubt will be surprising to many, and also be doubted by those who have not had an opportunity of knowing. I wish further to say that it quite frequently happens that the queen, when she fails to meet and copulate with a drone for twenty-one days, scarcely ever becomes fertilized, and will also commence laying eggs which produce drones only, and the whole colony will soon become extinct and have passed away. The drones n s being self-sustaining, likewise they have not the proper organs for fertilizing other queens, and soon perish, leaving no issue for a future generation.

Opinion of General Adair Doubted.

I am well aware that General Adair, of Hawesville, Kentucky, has a different opinion; for he asserted, in 1871, at the North American Bee Convention, held at Cleveland, Ohio, that he had a virgin which he had raised drones from, and that she became fertilized by her own offspring, which I cannot credit; or at least I feel certain that the General is laboring under a mistake, and believe I could account for the fertility of his virgin queen.

The drone is larger than the worker bee; has no sting, and therefore is harmless; is a consumer, and not a producer, of honey, pollen and water, and lives upon the labors of the industrious workers, and is unmercifully **expelled** from the hive after the swarming season is over.

(I have often thought I should very much dislike to be a drone.)

Now, dear reader, let me say to you, go to your bee-hive, if you have one you can open with ease, and learn lessons of wisdom; there is where we have a finer display of true Mother Nature than any man's pen can describe on paper. I have only opened up the way for a beginning for you, and am only sorry I have not the room in this little book to talk more to you, and lead you further into the fountain that is full of mystery, and will be as long as we live; but when you have there taken one lesson, it will fit you better for the second, and so on, until you in all probability will be made to exclaim, "Oh, what wonders to man there are in the little Honey-Bee and Nature's God!"

CHAPTER VII.

Driving Bees into New Hives.

I would here remark that this is a particular thing to do, especially so if you are not acquainted with the operation, yet it is also very simple, if properly understood. I have driven a full swarm from one hive into another in fifteen minutes, and not have a single person stung, or get stung myself. My plan is, first to take some warm water and sweeten it well with honey, or sugar will do, and sprinkle the bees with the syrup, and then take a roll of cotton rags and smoke them well (as mentioned in lesson on transferring), then carry them off to some cool and shady place, and turn your hive upside down, and set your new hive over the open end of the old stock to be driven. Now get you two good sized sticks, about eighteen inches long, and beat with the sticks on the sides of the hive with the bees in, and in a few minutes they will all go up and cluster as a regular swarm in the top of your new hive.

How to Locate Bees After Driving.

Place them in a new location, and the old hive you can set back at its old stand-point, where it will receive a sufficient number of workers to protect the brood, and will raise another queen. This driving process should always be done at the right time, or you may ruin your stocks. I have made four good, strong stocks from one in a season, and had them winter well, but it happened to be a good season.

How to Hive Bees and Settle Them When Allowed to Swarm.

If you prefer letting your bees swarm naturally, I would recommend a free use of water to be thrown among them while on the wing; first, if you have no bushes or fruit trees handy for them to settle on, I would say to get a few brushy-topped bushes and set them nearly where your bee-stands are, several days before you expect them to swarm; then, with a free use of water, as above, while they are on the wing, will generally settle them in due time. Now lose no time in making preparation to get them hived; which you can do very soon without much trouble. First, open the side door of your hive, if you have one of the Ilick's Hives, and place a small piece of board slanting edgewise, at the bottom of the hive, so your bees can have no trouble in going in; then before you undertake to do anything further, have you a pint or more of sweetened water, made quite sweet; with this gently sprinkle the swarm, and after you see they have commenced filling themselves, you can take the bushes and place them down close to the hive, and give the bush a quick jar with your hand, which will leave the bees about all at the base of your hive. (Don't be afraid of them, for I tell you, dear reader, they will not hurt you; this is why I have told you to sprinkle them with sweetened water.) Take a little brush broom, or a goose-quill is best, and brush them in gently; after which close up your door, and set them where you intend them to stand.

CHAPTER VIII.

On Patent or Movable Frame Hives.

This is a subject that perhaps may not interest you, my reader, very much; and

I can also say, that I can well recollect when I first heard of the reaper and mower; it was pronounced by many of our forefathers to be a humbug of Yankee origin, and yet, how is the farming business carried on? I leave you to judge. But improvement is now the order of the day, and he who will not keep up, must stay behind, for I claim that there are many advantages obtained, as well as a radical changes being made, in the management and culture of the honey-bee, as in any other branch of agriculture. Never did our fathers or mothers take from a single stand of bees in one season 328 pounds of nice honey, until they obtained and used a movable frame hive. And let me further say, that the above amount is no uncommon thing now; and even from 500 to 900 pounds have been taken in good, nice, extracted honey from a single stand of bees in one season. I have taken 152 pounds of nice extracted honey from a single stock of Italian bees, and made right good, strong stocks besides, which I sold at twenty-five dollars each in my hive, and my honey at forty-five cents per pound. This may seem rather fishy, as used to be said by those who doubted

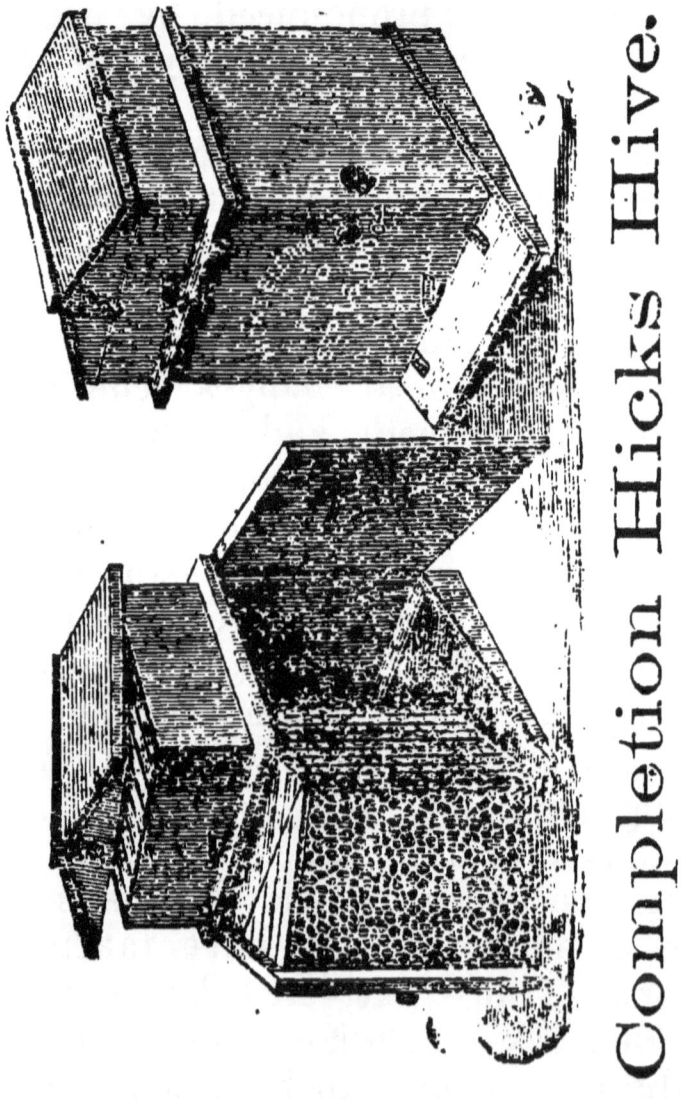

Completion Hicks Hive.

a report of any kind, when they thought it uncommon; but I have living witnesses who lived on an adjoining lot, and saw for themselves. I lived in the city of Indianapolis at the time, where there are many who know me.

Completion Hicks Bee-Hive.

It was in Indianapolis I lived when I completed my Bee-Hive and took out letters patent, in 1870, after working nearly twenty years on a plan to have a movable frame hive work to my own, as well as to the satisfaction of many others. This I truly believe I have accomplished, and feel certain that a man or woman can take care of at least one-third more stocks in the Hicks Bee-Hive than in any other ever invented and placed before the *bee-keeping world* for sale. I have used, and tried to use, some twenty different movable frame hives, but have never in any other hive procured as many advantages as in the Hicks Bee-Hive, having thoroughly tested it side by side with the Buckeye and Rough-and-Ready hives, both invented by N. C. Mitchell, the first of which I bought more square miles of territory in, than any other man that ever bought of the patentee; the last hive is not, nor ever was, patented, and yet I see agents making efforts to sell Rough-and-Ready Bee-Hives, and rights for the same.

Frauds Should be Put Down.

I apprehend that many who have made purchases in said hive last mentioned, would like to see the inventor or his agent. I have also come in contact at fairs of various counties with the Kidder and American Bee-Hives, in competition, and have as yet been successful over both of the last named, as well as over the Langstroth and Wilkinson Bee-Hives, at every fair where I have met them.

The Hicks Bee-Hive is one of the Easiest Hives to Handle Bees in

That has ever been placed before, or offered to bee-keepers of this country. Time will in the future, as well as it has in the past, speak out and tell the truth as to what hive is best for all general purposes in bee-keeping. The Hicks Hive has only to be seen in order to understand it, and tried to be appreciated. In it you can see at a glance any or all trouble, in which your bees need assistance. No frames to be removed by lifting out, but they can be all swung at one motion, which gives the keeper full control over the whole brood at once, and can examine each frame free and independent of any other, thereby rendering bee-keeping pleasant, as well as very profitable; it being so arranged that artificial swarms are made up in five minutes' time, and prevents the great loss by natural swarming, as they often go to the woods when allowed to swarm the old-fashioned way. In a word, it is the hive in which if you find weak stocks you can strengthen by changing a few frames with any other hive of the same pattern, or feed at any time, either winter or summer, without any danger of robbing by other bees; also, if a queen is to be found, it can be done in one minute, without lifting out a frame, or hurting a single bee in opening and closing the hive. Last, though not least, a lady or child can at any time take the surplus honey for table use or market, without coming in contact with the bees, or in any way interfering with the brood-chamber. (See cut of Hive, open and closed, shown both ways, on page 54.)

Vexed Question About Drones Explained.

In this article I propose to advance my own ideas concerning drones produced by a virgin queen, or a fertile worker, which I have never heard or read in any work on apiculture, or explained by any one; and why it is that a man as old in the bee business as Mr. Quinby, and who has written, perhaps, as much on bees as any one author in America, has never even tried to explain this subject about such drones, is a mystery to me; and yet, I hold it as a fact that all drones that are thus produced by such mothers are wholly worthless, and have not the proper functions, or in other words, they do not have the male organ properly developed, with which to fertilize a virgin queen, and are a perfect set of neuters, neither male or female.

Now let us examine a little, and see what the result will be. Suppose we have a stand of such drones in our apiary, and no other drones within four miles, and we have a good stock of bees with a good prolific mother; we now exchange a frame of worker brood with the fertile worker, or virgin queen stock, which are producing nothing but drones; the result is, the young bees thus placed in the said stock, will at once start queen-cells and raise a good virgin queen; and yet they are not any better off than before, from the fact that the drones are deficient, and cannot fertilize the young queen; but they will have exterminated the fertile worker, or the virgin queen, if such there is in the hive.

How Bees are Often Lost, and Cause Explained.

Now, dear reader, let me ask, if you do not recollect at any time in your life of a stand of bees being lost, and you did not know the cause, and often wondered why it was that the brood combs become so uneven, and looked as if something had been gnawing them, and almost made them look as if they had been cut into very roughly after the bees were all gone and but a few drones left to tell the tale of disaster? Let me here say to you, that nine times in ten you may set it down as a loss by having a virgin queen which has never become fertilized, or a fertile worker, which is worse, from the fact that you cannot hunt them out and destroy them, as you can the queen. I would therefore recommend you to hunt out and destroy all such virgin queens, when you discover such brood as above, which is very uneven, with raised cells, and perfectly haphazard—no regularity about it. But if you have no other queen to supply her place, then do as above, exchange a brood sheet from some good, prolific stock. I would also say, if it be that you are troubled with a fertile worker, which *I claim cannot be found and singled out*, you must also exchange a brood, comb, young bees and all, just as you find it, and my word for it, they will soon make a clearing out of said fertile worker, and raise a queen for themselves, which will save further trouble, if you have good and perfect drones in your apiary.

CHAPTER IX.

How to Raise Italian Drones Early.

First let me say, this requires some care, and must have some attention paid to it by the apiarian. You will first procure of some one (whom you can trust), a *pure Italian queen*, say in August or September, and see that you get her properly introduced into a good, strong and healthy stock of bees. Now when the winter sets in fairly, I would recommend you to put them in some quiet, warm and dark place, just cool enough to not freeze. See that they have plenty of honey to keep them at least three months before you put them away in their winter quarters. Now let me further say, you must take three or four pounds of honey to a quart of warm water, and let it stand in a tin vessel twelve hours, after which set it on a stove and bring to a boil and skim. Now feed about a half to a table-spoonful once a day from the 20th of February, until the weather gets warm enough to set them out on their proper stand for the season; feed in old combs placed in the top of Hicks Hive, which can be done at any time; my word for it, you will have drones one month earlier than your neighbor, who trusts to luck and allows his bees to swarm the old-fashioned way. (See artifical swarming.)

Be sure to feed as above directed, *every day*, until the bees gather plenty of pollen and honey for natural resources. You can also give a little rye meal as a substitute for pollen while feeding.

Introduction of Italian Queens— The Proper Manner of Introducing a Queen to a Full Colony of Bees.

First, find and capture the queen you desire to supercede, then cage her and leave the cage in the hive, say six or eight hours; then open your hive as quietly as possible, and take the queen out of the cage, and put your Italian queen in the same cage; cut a piece of honey to plug the hole with, and then set the cage carefully back in the hive, and the bees will soon liberate her, while they are left alone, which will be in five or six hours.

I have practiced this method some five or six years, and found it the best of many plans which I have tried, never having lost a single queen yet, with the above mode of operation, and think that all who tries it will have no cause to regret having purchased this book, as the above is worth ten times the cost.

How to Raise or Breed Queens.

First, select the stock you desire to breed from, and then divide the brood by placing two frames into hives you have made queenless eight or nine days previous, and thus exchange with, say three hives, first cutting out all queen-cells in the three queenless colonies, when the bees will go to work and build from six to twelve cells in each hive, which you can cut out of and insert into other stocks, on the eighth day, and thus Italianize some fifteen or twenty in a short time, letting each one raise its own queens.

How to Prevent Bees from Distroying their young, and the Cause.

This is a lesson of importance to every bee-keeper. First let me say, as a general rule, the destruction of young bees is caused from a scarcity of honey, which is also brought about by a cold spell of the weather, which closes up the flowers or bloom of the fields, and makes it hard work for bees to get a sufficient amount of honey to go on with the raising of their young, and sets them at once to destroying and carrying the young unmatured bees out, which we so often see lying in front of the hives, of a morning, when we first visit our apiary. This is the effect of such cool weather as we have in the month in May, and often in June. I have quite frequently seen heavy frosts in these two months which killed the flowers so that there was very little honey to be gathered by the bees; and rather than starve they would at once fall to work and destroy their young. Now, when you see this state of things going on, you *must* prevent it at once, by feeding as directed; except you will feed a double quantity of syrup in their case. Sometimes they will kill off their young rather than swarm, but this you can prevent by ariificial swarming, and make them yourself, and make many good, strong stocks by so doing, with an addition of a little feed. But if you desire to obtain honey, do not practice artificial swarming very extensively; but keep your stocks strong with plenty of empty surplus frames, as above, and out out all queen-cells.

Foul Broods—Cause of.

I have no doubt but that this disease is caused from impure honey and soured bee-bread, which has been stored quite early in the season by the bees. I think it is quite like every other kind of natnre's production, which is frequently gathered by the bees before it gets ripe or fully matured; and being stored away in close packages, as is the case, which we all know. They store bee-bread in the brood-combs near where the young bees are being raised, and there being so much animal heat necessary to keep up the proper temperature, it causes the farina, or bee-bread, which is gathered first, to become soured, with the honey also that they must use in preparing the food for the young larvæ, and this impure food must necessarily bring on disease, and is therefore called foul-brood.

Foul Brood—How Known.

It may very readily be known by its offensive smell, and on a close examination you will discover that the brood is inverted, dead, and seems to be all tail-foremost in the cells, rather dark and ropy-like mass. The best remedy I have ever found in treating this disease is a preparation prepared thus: take pure rain water and boil it ten minutes and to every gallon dissolve four pounds of A coffee sugar and again bring it to a boil and skim. Now to one quart of this syrup put in a lump of borax (biporate of soda) about as large as a medium sized hickory nut, and thoroughly dissolved while hot by stirring, and then let cool until about blood heat then add one oz. of laudinum, [tincture of opium] also one table spoonful of good table salt all to be well stirred before using, now take a fine brush broom and sprinkle over the combs gently once a day, cut out all the dead brood.

Dysentery, or Bee Cholera.

This is also one of the most to be dreaded diseases that the bee-keeper has to contend with. It is met with more frequently than any other among bees. It is very easy to distinguish it from any other malady, yet I do not think it contagious as many suppose it to be. The bees have a tendency to be rather dauncy and also have a very unpleasant odor. When you approach a stand affected with dysentery they mope or crawl slowly over their combs and often coming out and discharge their excrement over the hive as well as over their brood combs and honey and if let alone often linger out a miserable life. In fact there are more bees lost in North America with this disease annually, than all the rest of the diseases known to bees. It is quite unpleasant to have a case of this kind, and in fact it is not pleasant to meet with a diseased subject of any kind, either in the animal or human family.

Treatment of Bee Cholera.

But like either of the last mentioned races I claim it can be successfully treated when we find a colony troubled with this complaint. The first thing to do is to take the stand to some quiet warm place and open them out gently so as not to get them to flying and have you some good syrup, made of honey if possible, boiling with a pint of good nice rain water to two pounds of honey, and skim it well, so as to take off all impurities, and let cool, so that you can now put one table-spoonful in some old bits of comb laid in your hive, and the bees will come up and feed on this syrup. Feed the above amount once a day regularly, when in a few days you can set them.

CHAPTER X.

The Italian Bees, and Their Superiority over the Common Native Bee.

Let me here say that the description of this class or race of bees has so often been explained heretofore that I hardly deem it necessary to enter into a full detail, but suffice it to say that all who have tested their qualities as workers universally acknowledge them as being far ahead of the native or common bees of this country. In the first place, they are more friendly disposed toward their keeper, and can be handled with more pleasure, and less danger of being stung, while it is acknowledged by all that they are by far better honey gatherers; also, they are larger than the Black Bees, and defend their hives from robbers better, and, in a word, let me say I have yet to hear of a colony of pure Italians ever being taken with the *pest*, called the moth worms; while we, as bee-keepers, can not say the same for the native class we have had and tested over a century in this country. The Italian queens being of a very beautiful golden color, are more easily found in a hive or swarm, and are more prolific than black queens are, which give their keeper larger and stronger swarms earlier in the season, so that we can be more certain of getting a generous supply of honey, if native fields, with their millions of bloom, secrete the nectar for them to work on. This class, called the Italian Bees, were discovered during the wars of Napoleon by Captain Boldenstein, who brought them over the Alps in 1843. They were also introduced by a celebrated German bee-keeper, in 1853, into Germany, and in 1860 into the United States. I should say more in their favor, but I fear some one will at once say that Hicks is grinding his ax for the sale of queens; but be this as it may, let me say to you, brother bee-keeper, that if you once try the pure Italian Bees, you would not give one stock for two of our old-fashioned natives, which we first procured as seed from the woods. I have them as pure as they are in Italy, and am better pleased every day with them; and if you would come to my apiary you would be convinced the same as I am. I could here give many names as references who have procured queens of me who have universally spoke in praise of the Italian Bees as being by far superior to the old-fashioned kind; they also work on red clover in August. While the honey harvest is scarce they seem to be busy on many dark and misty days, while the black bees are idle, and using up their already scanty supply.

How to Italianize a Hundred Stands with One Queen, and Leave Her in the Same Hive.

After you have a good queen introduced, as before stated [see lesson on introducing Italian queen to bees], you will, as soon as she is laying eggs freely, go and kill, say about four bees in your black stock, and in eight days go to them again, open and examine carefully and cut out all queen cells. Then you can take out one frame of each hive and brush the bees back into their own hives. Now go to your Italian stock, and take four frames; brushing the bees off into their own hive, and put in the four from the other stocks, and give each black stock a frame from the Italian brood from which they will raise queens from the fresh eggs, pure Italian, and if you have other black stock you can also go and kill their queens, and in eight days you can cut out part of the queen's cells and divide them by inserting the combs, which will save much precious time.

What is Pollen, and Why Bees Use it for Food.

In this lesson we shall perhaps differ greatly from most bee-keepers. Pollen is the fecundating dust of plants, and is of a mealy like substance, which bees of all classes seem to have a special desire for, and especially so with the honey bee as it is well known by all persons who keep them, that they gather and carry into their hives in large quantities, of which it is said they use during winter as food; but my experience has taught me to respect this idea of theirs so far only as the young bees are concerned, which are under fourteen days old, after being hatched, and before they become outside workers, for it is during their minority that they are the nurse-bees in the hive, as well as they are the wax-workers the first thirty days of their active life in gathering honey, pollen and water for supplies, after which they perform such other duties as are necessary about the hive, in guarding and defending that which they have spent the best part of their lives for. Dear reader, let me once more say to you that the worker bee does not live over fifty days from the time it commences its labors as a honey gatherer. It is also my opinon that the older bees are the ones that bring in what is known as propolis or bee-glue, of which they use large quantities to close up cracks and openings in their hives. This pollen is bread for the young and tender bees that are performing duty in the hive, in preparing food for the young yet unhatched, and also, it is my opinion, which I feel certain, is quite correct, that it is those bees that are always most busy in cleaning cells from which bees are constantly hatching.

How to Feed Weak Stocks in Order to Save Them.

This will be a job deserving of some care; but while it has been my misfortune to meet with many such in my travels among bee-keepers, I will here give my method, which I have found nine times in ten to prove effectual. If you have honey, I would recommend it to be used, but if not, then sugar will do by preparing it thus: Take rain water and heat it to a boil, after which put into a quart of water four pounds of A coffee sugar, or, if honey is to be used, put in six pounds of honey, stir well until it again boils, and then skim off all impurities, and let cool. Now you can take some bits of old combs, and pour a spoonful or two on the same, and place in the top of or on the hive, so the bees can come up and take it all down. If it is in the winter, set your hive in a warm room, where there will be no noise or confusion, feed regular every day for ten or fifteen days. This mode will save many stocks that would otherwise be lost. It will pay to feed all such stocks.

Old Fogies Must Succumb.

But, says one old fogy, if I have to do all this, I would rather let them go. Yes, my old friend, your ideas are just what has got most bee-keepers in past ages to believe it is all in luck, when, in fact, it is science. Will you attend to it? Let me here suggest that when you have a pig, or a calf, cow or horse that has met with some accident, and got down, as the saying is, at the heel, would you let them go? I rather guess not, but would at once proceed to doctor them up, and reap your reward in the future by the increase of its value. Therefore let me impress it upon you to attend to your bees at once, when you can so easily do so by following the directions laid down in this little book.

Advice to Beginners in Apiculture.

I will here say a few words to those who contemplate going into the business of keeping bees as a means of making a living at it, which, I apprehend will be many, when I shall have gone, and not return this way any more. First, let me say that February or March are the best months in which to make your purchases of stocks; and don't always choose the heaviest as best, but rather select those with good bright combs and a sufficiency of honey to last two months. Also let me say, if you desire to succeed in the business, you must adopt a good movable frame hive, and get you a neat and well made sample, by which you will also make or have made all the hives you may need for a year, just like the sample hive, and have them all painted two good coats of paint and oil. Then, when the bees are about to swarm, I would have all the stocks transferred into your new hives, and in all probability you can have an increase of one-third by your operation of transferring, if you are careful and understand what you are doing. [See lesson on transferring.] It will be necessary that you look at your bees by opening the hives at least once or twice a week, and if you should discover any moth-worms, take them out of the brood combs with a sharp-pointed knife, also, don't fail to put your foot on every worm, and send it to its long home. Don't try to do too much the first year, as here is where many make failures in starting out with big ideas, and finally pronounce the business a humbug. But let me say there is no surer way in all the agricultural pursuits than the business, and yet it may be badly managed, and prove almost ruinous to those who neglect its demands, and finally the next we hear of them is that they pronounce it all in luck, and wind up with perhaps many dollars out of pocket. And yet I know of hundreds who have made it a success, and some of them have made fortunes. It is a business in which both old and young can engage, and make it a success if they will put their energies to work with a will and determination to go through. I know of two young ladies, sisters, who made nearly seven thousand dollars in one year; and yet they live in the cold and bleak State of Wisconsin. I will further add that there is scarcely any place in the United States so poor but there can be a few stands of bees kept to advantage, while almost any person could and can keep bees, which will yield a larger income than any other stock can possibly do with the same cost and expense. It is also a fact that no one dare gainsay that bees will pay better dividends on the capital invested than United States bonds of any class or series, and better than any railroad, canal, turnpike or gravel road coporation have or will ever pay in this country. Not even the banking business can begin to pay such dividends as bees well managed pay their owners. I know that many will say I have gone wild on this subject; but here allow me to say I know of a gentleman in Northwestern Indiana who made five hundred dollars in one season from one stand of bees in his door-yard.

Each Month's Labors Laid Out for the Apiary.

MARCH—This is the month you should see that all your bees have a generous supply, and if the weather is warm you should set them on their regular stands for the season.

APRIL—Examine and see that they feed plentiful; also be careful and set all your hives where you intend them to remain, keep a cover over all your stocks; also, if they are not gathering pollen, give rye bread.

MAY—Examine carefully, and see that all stocks have a prolific queen, and that no robbing is going on.

JUNE—In this month you should supply the surplus chamber with frames or boxes, and give them all the combs you can to fill with surplus honey, and if you don't wish swarming, cut out all the queen cells.

JULY—If you desire so to do, now is your time for transferring and making up a few extra colonies; if not, keep plenty of frames or boxes supplied for others to store surplus honey in.

AUGUSTT—Now is the greatest time for trouble with the robbers. Keep the entrances closed, so that a single bee can pass out and in at a time. Also be careful about the moth-worm, and be sure to kill all you see.

SEPTEMBER—Now is the time that you should keep all your stocks strong in numbers, and see well to it that they all have good prolific queens. It is also a good month to procure Italian queens.

OCTOBER—Is good, also, to introduce queens, and guard well against moth-worms; also see that you keep your bees in good condition.

NOVEMBER—In this month equalize your bees, and take away all honey from the caps, but leave plenty in the brood chamber, so they will be supplied through the winter.

DECEMBER—This is the first winter month, and is the proper time to hive your bees; if the weather gets cold so as to freeze the ground quite hard, close up all lower ventilation when you put them in your bee hive, cellar or cave, which should have plenty of upper ventilation;

the hives must have upper ventilation; keep the temperature at about 35 deg. above zero, and keep the place you have your bees stored in very dark and quiet. If the winter should be very open and warm, I would recommend to leave them on their summer stands, and fill the top of your hives with dry cobs or fine cut straw, made quite dry.

JANUARY—This is the month in which have all the hives you need for the coming year made and well painted, which will be in readiness for swarming season or artificial division, which is by far the best where you use a good frame hive,.

FEBRUARY—See well to it that your bees are well supplied with honey, and if you have any stocks from which you expect to breed queens and drones, you should feed a little syrup about the 20th of this month. [See lesson on feeding bees—weak stocks.]

'Last, though not least, I will here once more impress it upon you to be prompt in all your undertakings with bees, and do everything in due season, as per advice, and success is yours, with a rich reward for all your troubles; also, it is a true saying whatever is worth doing at all is worth doing well.

On Choosing a Location for an Apiary.

In making your selection, let me say, choose an east view, so your hives may have the benefit of the early morning rays of the sun to enliven them to early action in gathering honey and pollen, all of which is necessary to the welfare of your bees, as well, also, as to the keeper. If the above position or situation cannot be obtained, or something as near as possible, I would, as a next best choice, take a south front, but by no means allow your stands to receive the noonday sun, as this would be detrimental, quite often causing the combs to melt down and destroy your bees, as well as your honey, and set bees to robbing.

How to Build a Bee House.

Now, dear reader, let me tell you how I build a bee house, one that any farmer, as well as the more polished mechanic, can build quite cheap. Set two rows of posts, say about six feet apart in one row, and in the other twelve feet apart, and eight feet apart in the last mentioned row, and in the first let your posts be about six feet above ground, and cut them off on a line quite level, and spike poles or scantling on top to rest your rafters on; then spike a scantling about six inches above the ground on your lowest row of posts, which now prepares it for siding, like a barn, on one side, then put on a good roof of clapboard or plank; this constitutes your bee house. You can arrange your bees under this shed so the hives will front eastward and to the open side of your shed, which is all sufficient for summer use, remembering always to set the hives about three inches clear of the ground by driving four small stakes down, and leveling them so the hive will stand quite plumb. Let the hives stand about eighteen inches clear of each other, remembering, also, to have them painted of different colors. and set alternate, 'no two of the same shade side by side, which will, if practiced as I have suggested, save many valuable queens for you in the course of a season.

Pasturage for Bees.

I would next recommend you and all the rest of mankind to sow seeds of various kinds, such as Alsyke clover, white clover, plant trees and shrubs of various kinds, as they will be useful for bees, as well as for man and beast, producing the best of pasturage for stock, and hay for feeding your cattle, sheep and horses during winter; especially the Alsyke clover can not be excelled for hay, as well as for honey. It stands ahead of all other. There are many trees I might here mention as shade and fruit trees, of which the linden or basswood is first, poplar maple, elm, buckeye or horse-chestnut, also, the yellow willow is fine for bees, together with apple, peach, pear, plumb, apricot, nectarine, cherry, quince, and I would not forget the black locust; also, there are many small shrubs which are of value, such as currant, gooseberry, raspberry and blackberry, of which I need not mention further, as they are common to almost all who have any knowledge of farming or gardening, and are all good for honey.

CHAPTER XI.

Bee Stings, and Remedies for the Same.

I will here give a cure for bee sting. As soon as you are stung procure a good sized padlock key, fill the barrel about half full of soda and salt mixed, then fill up with water, or cider vinegar is better, then apply the key over the wound with the solution on the part so as to cover where the sting was extracted, which should always be done first with your finger nail or knife blade.

Another Simple and Sure Remedy

That all persons have at their fingers-end is to first extract the sting as soon as possible, as before stated, with your nail or knife-blade, then wet the end of your finger in your mouth, and then insert it in your ear, so as to get wax from what we might call a dirty ear, and rub on the wound, which will give relief quite soon. This is a sure and positive cure, which we all have at any time and place we happen to be. It sometimes happens that persons get badly stung, and that it makes them very sick, causing terrible swelling, blindness, and excruciating pain. In all such cases I would recommend a free use of salt water as a wash, abundantly applied to the parts stung, and a cup of warm water, with a table-spoonful of mustard, well stirred in as an emetic, which must be drank at once, so as to produce vomiting as soon as possible. This will relieve in severe cases.

The Profits of Bee-keeping Compared with that of Other Stocks.

In this article I propose to show you, dear reader, that there is no other investment that will begin to pay the profits to the owner that bees will if properly and fairly managed, yet how often is it that persons will try to snub you, and turn up their noses and say "It is too small a business for me," when, if you were to take the trouble to investigate the profits they reap year after year, you would find that you, with ten stands of bees properly managed, would reap a larger income in one year than that man or woman who is afraid of getting into the small business of bee-keeping. For instance, let us look, and contrast one stand of bees and the profits of the same with that of a sheep for one or two years. We will allow, say five dollars for the sheep, and the same for the bees, which I think is a fair price. Now for the result. The bees will have, say one extra stand, as they, no doubt, will swarm (which I would much prefer—artificial swarming), and you will, of an ordinary season, get, say forty pounds of honey to the stand, worth thirty cents per pound. This would bring you twenty-four dollars, and your extra swarm is worth five dollars more; in all it would be twenty-nine dollars. Deducting the cost of hive, say two dollars, would leave you twenty-seven dollars clear profit. Now what has the sheep made all this time? for I wish to be fair, and give due credits where they belong. Well, in the first place, it is worth three dollars a year to feed the sheep, and say we now have a lamb six months old, worth two dollars and fifty cents for wool and lamb, which leaves only fifty cents as profit, to say nothing about time and trouble of feeding both winter and summer, while your bees have boarded themselves and made you a clear gain of twenty-seven dollars. But, says some doubting Thomas, this will do to talk about and show on paper. Well, Mr. T., I propose to more than double this with my bees, and will here challenge any man to try me on ten or twenty stands of bees, and he to take the same number of sheep, and if I will not double his profits in one or ten years, he shall have all I make from the bees, if he will do the same by me and give me all his sheep, with their increase, at the end of said term if I beat him.

A Mystery Much Doubted by Other Authors.

I have often forced a colony of bees to make queens by taking their queen from them, which they at once proceeded to supply as soon as they discover their mother queen missing, and it often happens that when their young queen has hatched out and become fully of age to meet the drone, she will make her bridal tour, and is lost by some accident—high winds, or a bird may catch her before she reaches her home again. This, I say, is often the case, which should always keep the bee-keeper on the lookout, and to know the exact condition of every hive of bees in his apiary; and if he should find a stock of bees thus made queenless, it demands his immediate attention, and he should have one or two frames of brood with eggs exchanged from some other strong stock, in order that they may again make a queen for themselves. Now comes the mysterious part. You will often find queen cells built on one or more of their old combs in which there could not have been a single egg, except it was transferred from one of the combs which you gave them with eggs and brood. How came they to build a queen cell on a sheet of comb of their own when there could not have been an egg in it, except by transfer from one comb to another? Oh, says one, they had eggs of their own. Now, my dear reader, here let me say this can not be so, from the fact that bees do make their queens from eggs that are laid or deposited by a fertile queen in the worker cells, and they can not be thus converted or transferred into a royal queen after they are seven days old. Hence you will discover that during the time required to hatch the queen that was lost on the bridal trip would have been some twenty-four or five days up to the time you discovered your stock was queenless, and gave them the frames of brood, as above referred to. I apprehend that the theory, as taught by many writers, about the queen depositing the egg in the royal cell is false, and can not be relied on as being correct; and that the worker bees, which are not more than fourteen days old, are the managers of all that pertains to the welfare of the inside arrangements of the hive, I have no doubt, for we see them, as I have before remarked, enter on their duties from the moment they are hatched out of their cells. I think I have said enough upon this point, and shall leave the student to his observatory hive for further instructions, which will be of more value to you than all I could write in an age; yet this will serve to give you a start.

Inverted Brood, and What is the Result.

I here wish, for the purpose of drawing from others, if possible, their views as to the true cause of the young bees being raised or nearly matured in their cells, with their posteriors in front of cells, which I have often seen, and can not account for such a state of affairs. Would it not be reasonable to suppose that this would cause foul brood, which is so much dreaded by bee-keepers? It is my humble opinion this state of things would naturally be inclined to produce said disease, from the fact that it would be impossible for them to hatch with their heads toward the center of the comb and the tail outwards, which must produce death before they are fully matured, and a perfect ropy mass will be the result, which, with the animal heat of the older bees, causes a putrid and offensive smell, which is not pleasant to the apiarian or visitor, and to be loathed by all who may come in contact with it. I have often seen such brood, and I think, without exception, foul brood ensued if they were not taken out in due time. I desire the opinions of others as to the true cause, if any other there be. Let me hear from any one who is well posted on the subject of foul brood.

Who may Keep Bees and Make Them Pay.

In connection with the above subject, I might say a great deal, and many things that would tickle the mind, as well as make you feel quite certain that

God never made a man, woman or child who had arrived at a proper age of discretion but could keep bees. But while I claim this to be true, I also know that there are many who are too indolent and careless to even keep themselves, mutch less take care of a few stands of bees. And yet, notwithstanding, I might add that the poor, as well as the rich, can make bee-keeping quite profitable. Then let me further say, the farmer, the mechanic or the lawyer, as well as the doctor who may have a few moments to spare morning and evening, may keep a few stands of bees, as well as the poor washerwoman, or a lady with her thousands of dollars can make bee-keeping a success, and have upon her table one of nature's richest and choisest of luxuries at a very small expense. I may also add to the list very many ministers of the gospel, who have worn themselves out in the service of the ministry. and have been superannuated on account of poor health. To all such let me say, try bee-keeping. If you but try you will become interested in the business, and make it pay. I would not forget, also, the poor consumptive, who needs out-door exercise in order to get pure air for his or her lungs, with that of moderate exercise for the body. To all such as mentioned let me say, if you are poor from, and have been in the service of the Gospel, standing as a superannuated minister, I will let you have one of my hives, with bees in the same, at half price, and give you the right to make and use all you may want thereafter.

I will now talk to the ladies a little. And first allow me to say that when they become interested in the bee business they make the best of apiarians, from the fact that they take more pains in the handling of their bees than men do, and it is, in the very nature of things, adapted to their nature and disposition, for there is nothing that loves kind treatment better than a swarm of bees, which ladies are always ready to bestow. Furthermore, they attend more closely and strictly to their work, which is the only sure road to success, as it begets industrious and steady habits. If we could induce the young and rising generation to pay more attention to bee-keeping, and not so much to the flippant styles of fashion, we would have a better class of men and women, and fewer paupers and convicts in our asylums, penitentiaries and county jails.

How to Winter Bees Successfully.

In this lesson I will give the most approved plan, at least the one I like best. In the first place, let me say, never put your bees away in their winter quarters until the weather has become settled cold and the ground has frozen quite hard. Then you can put them in a cellar, if it is a dry one, but if not let me entreat you to prepare a house with double walls, so that you can fill the space with spent tanbark, or sawdust will do; at any rate, prepare a house that will prevent freezing, as it requires, a great deal more honey to winter out in the open air than it does in a place that is dry and will not freeze. After you have thus prepared suitable winter quarters, you can now set your bees in carefully, not jarring them in handling, and place the stands, say about six inches apart, leaving plenty of upper ventilation; also, be careful that mice do not enter any of the stocks and cut the combs, as well as kill many of the bees. It is a well known fact that the wood mice are death to bees, and often destroy a whole swarm in a few days. You must keep your cellar, or bee house (as the case may be), cool enough, so that the bees will not become restless; also, warm enough so that it will not freeze; the proper temperature is about 35 degrees above zero, and if dry, you will have no trouble in wintering safely through.

How to Keep Honey from Souring,

This may be done either of two ways or modes. The first is to boil and skim thoroughly, and put away in good earthen or glass jars, and cover up closely. In this way I have kept, and have known others to keep, honey several years. But if you desire to keep your honey so as to retain all its original flavor, you will let it stand a few hours in an open vessel, and then warm it up to about blood heat, which will cause all impurities to come to the top, which you will take off gently with a large spoon or fine skimmer, then jar and can as you would fruit, which will also keep for five years and be good.

To Keep Honey from Granulating.

You must boil gently thirty minutes, and skim off all impurities, and place away in ordinary jars, and keep covered with paper, or a cloth will do, when kept close, to keep out all dust or insects.

To Make Taffy from Honey for the Children.

Let me say this is one of the most healthy and best of candies for our little folk, which can be prepared thus: Take, say a quart of good strained honey and cook it in a skillet, or an oven such as our mothers used to bake the good old-fashioned corn dodger in, and put into it a small lump of alum half the size of a small hickory nut, and boil until it begins to make wax, which you can test by having a cup of cold water, and with a spoon drop a few drops into it, and you can soon judge of its qualities, which, when sufficiently hard to suit, you may now take pie-pans and butter them before pouring the taffy in, after which pull, and use as best suits your taste.

What is Honey Dew, and How is It Produced?

I do not wish to go into a long detailed story, but shall proceed at once to give my own views, which I believe are as near correct as anything I have ever read upon the subject; hence, if I should reiterate in part the views of any former opinion expressed, it will only be so far as I shall coincide with some of the expressions that have come under my especial notice. But feeling that all is not true that has been or yet remains to be written, I shall therefore give you, dear readers, what I feel assured are facts, so far as I have been able to gather them. Hence, when we take into account the mysteries that Nature's God has brought about to produce and perfect her work in all the vegetable, as well as the animal and insect kingdoms, I feel like saying that honey dew is also one of the many mysteries that man is not yet fully acquainted with. But when we look back to days that have passed and gone, we can fully recollect that honey dews always come when the weather is warm and pleasant, and the trees and shrubs all dressed in living green; likewise, the flowers are out in full bloom, and that we behold all nature smiling in her beauty. Then it is that we see, of a beautiful, bright morning, the leaves of many and various kinds of bushes fairly glistening with that sweet nectar called honey dew. Hence, I believe it to be secreted in the many and various flowers through the night, and, by the chemical action of the sun of those warm days, it is taken up into the atmosphere in a condensed form, and then returns to the earth in a liquid, lodging upon the shrubs and trees in the night time, and is one of the richest harvests for our bees. In other words, it is the rich odor of flowers and plants thrown off in the day time that is thus returned in the sweet-like substance sometimes so bountifully bestowed for the good of man. It also feeds many thousands of insects, and supports many colonies of bees. But, as is often said, many who profess that there is an insect, called aphis, producing honey dews, as we commonly understand the term, I do not believe; yet I am well aware that there are such insects, and tree and bud lice, that suck the juice of the tender leaves and buds of various shrubs, and will exude a substance similar to honey dews; but surely we could not be so foolish as to believe it to be honey dew of the regular order.

A Visit to the North American Bee-keepers Convention in 1871.

It has been my province to examine several works on this drone question as to purity, and I claim that it is a fixed fact in nature that the drone is effected in its purity, as well as the workers of all queens that may become fertilized by black drones, is certainly reasonable, and why Mr. Kretchmer, who has published two different books on bee-keeping, should say that all drones from an Italian queen which has been fertilized by a black drone are pure is certainly a stretch in a direction that takes nature's laws down, as well as natural science. [See last edition, page 125.] And again, when he, in the same book, page 126, states that the drones vary in color more than queens or workers, I suppose he has direct reference to the Italian drones; if so, I do not wonder at such discrepancies, and must say to you, friend Kretchmer, I do not wish to make any purchases of your so-called Italian pure stock. I feel that all such theories should and will be put down as the people become more enlightened on the subject; and while I think of it, let me say that in 1871, while I attended the North American Bee-keepers' Convention at Cleveland, Ohio, it afforded me much pleasure to hear the different views of many who professed to be well posted on the drone question, one of whom was a doctor Bowyer, of Alexandria, Indiana, and who had the starch all taken out of him by that old and venerable sage, doctor and professor, Curtland, a man for whom I entertain the highest respect, and give great credit to his views, who boldly asserted before the entire convention that it was certain that a pure blood was tainted by cohabiting with another or mixed race, and that it would hold good in the insect as well as the animal or human creation, and I believe especially so where the female is of pure blood of a different class. Now, it is admitted by all that the Italian bee is of a different class and of a superior race to that of the black bee of this country, and when the two races are brought together and bred as above spoken of, it will effect the entire family, and continue to do so as long as that mother queen raises bees or drones that fertilize your young queens. I would, therefore, advise you, dear reader, to be careful in making your purchases. If you desire to get pure stock and keep them so, you will first have to get that which is pure, and then breed as directed and laid down in this book, and success will crown your efforts. [See lesson Page 61. How to Raise Italian drones.]

I can not refrain from giving friend Quinby a passing notice, who claims to have raised virgin queens late in the fall for the purpose of having early drones the next spring. [See his second edition, page 37.] I do not miss my guess very much when I say to him, that so far as such drones are concerned, they are wholly worthless, and never were known to fertilize a queen at any time of the year, and I doubt his or any one else ever wintering such a stock over.

[See pages 28, 29 and 30, this Book.]

INDEX.

	PAGE.
The Natural History and Description of the Honey Bee,	1
Drones are Larger than the Worker Bees—More About the Worker Bee	2
Size and Shape of Queens	5
Age of Queens Not Certain—A Test of Queens Laying Eggs	6
Do Queens Sting	7
Construction of Royal Cells	8
Impregnation of the Queen	10
Artificial Fertilization in Confinement	11
How a Fertile Queen is Known	12
How a Virgin Queen or Drone-Laying Queen is Known—An Instance of Two Queens in One Hive	13
The Impregnating or Seminal Fluid	14
On Swarming, and Why Bees Swarm—First Swarm	16
The Old Queen Going with Them	18
When the First Swarm is Cast—The P'ping of the Queens	19
Queens Do Often Meet in Mortal Combat	21
What a Queen Cell Looks Like	23
What A Royal Queen Cell is Made of	25
Do Bees Supercede Their Queens	26
Further Explanation of Sex	28
On Transferring Bees and Brood into Movable Frame Hives	31
Why is it that Bees of the Present Day do not Swarm so Much nor Make as Much Honey as They Did Years Ago, During the Early Settlement of the Country	33
Do Queens Have a Sting? And if so, Do They Ever Use Them, and What On?	37
More Persons than do Should Keep Bees	39
Artificially Swarming Bees	42
A Fertile Worker—How Known	44

How to Get Rid of the Fertile Worker—On the Drone Question, and What the Drone is For......................... 46
Opinion of General Adair Doubted 48
Driving Bees into New Hives.. 49
How to Locate Bees After Driving................................ 50
How to Hive Bees and Settle Them When Allowed to Swarm.. 51
On Patent or Movable Frame Hives............................... 52
Competition of the Hicks Bee-Hive................................ 55
Frauds Should be Put Down—The Hicks Bee-Hive is One of the Easiest Hives to Handle Bees in................. 56
Vexed Question About Drones Explained...................... 58
How Bees are Often Lost, and Cause Explained........... 59
How to Raise Italian Drones Early................................. 61
Introduction of Italian Queens—The Proper Manner of Introducing a Queen to a Full Colony of Bees........... 62
How to Raise or Breed Queens...................................... 63
How to Prevent Bees from Destroying Their Young, and the Cause... 64
Foul Brood—Cause of... 65
Foul Brood—How Known... 66
Dysentery, or Bee Cholera... 67
Treatment of Bee Cholera.. 68
The Italian Bees, and Their Superiority Over the Common Native Bee.. 69
How to Italianize a Hundred Stands with One Queen, and Leave Her in the Same Hive.............................. 71
What is Pollen, and Why Bees Use it for Food............. 72
How to Feed Weak Stocks in Order to Save Them...... 74
Old Fogies Must Succumb.. 75
Advice to Beginners in Apiculture................................ 76
Each Month's Labors Laid Out for the Apiary.............. 79
On Choosing a Location for an Apiary—How to Build a Bee-house.. 82
Pasturage for Bees.. 84
Bee Stings, and Remedies for the Same—Another Simple and Sure Remedy... 85
The Profits of Bee-Keeping Compared with that of Other Stock... 86
A Mystery Much Doubted by Other Authors................ 89
Inverted Brood, and What is the Result....................... 91
Who May Keep Bees and Make Them Pay................... 92
How to Winter Bees Successfully.................................. 95
How to Keep Honey from Souring................................ 96
To Keep Honey from Granulating—To Make Talley for the Children... 97
What is Honey Dew, and How is It Produced............. 98
A Visit to the North American Bee-Keepers' Convention in 1871..100

ERRATA.

The first word in the last line of introductory remarks should read "laws," in place of "was."

The first word in last line on page 43 should read "some," and not "same." Also, on page 51, in lesson "How to Hive Bees," the word "nearly," in the seventh line, should read "near by." On page 53, third line from bottom, the first word should read "eight," in place of "right." Also, the letter "o" in last word in twenty-first line from top of page should be "c," and read as "nice." On pages 54 and 55, the word "Completion" should read "Competition of the Hicks Bee-hive," and not "Completion Hicks Hive." On page 62, fifteenth line, the word "for" should read "from; and on page 64 the word "in" should be "of," in fifth line from bottom, after "month." Also, the last word on page 66 should be "bicarbonate," in place of "biporate." On page 69, the second line should have the words "back on their stand" supplied, in order to make the lesson clear and comprehensive in the treatment of bee cholera. On page 70, the word "native," in twelfth line from top, should read "nature," and on page 71 we find in third line from bottom the word "bees," which should be "queens;"—"stocks," in second line from bottom, should be "stacks. Also, on page 72, line 14, the word "in" should be used after "inserting," to make sense. On page 77, line sixteen, just before "business" should be "this business." On page 79, in lesson for April, the word "have" should be used before "feed," to make proper sense; and "meal" should be used in place of "bread." On page 80, the word "hive," in December lesson, should be "house," which is used in second and sixth lines.

Price List of

HIVES, BEES

AND

ITALIAN QUEENS,

At Retail and by the Quantity.

SINGLE COPY OF THE

North American Bee-keeper's Guide.................................$	50
Hicks' Bee Hive and Farm Right.................................	10 00
Hicks' Bee Hive, with Italian Bees..............................	20 00
For Hicks' Hives per dozen..	36 00
Italian Queen, single one tested................................	5 00
Italian Queens per dozen..	33 00
Italian Queens per half dozen....................................	18 00
One imported Italian Queen......................................	10 00
Alsike Clover Seed per pound...................................	50
Mustard Seed per pound...	35
Silver-hulled Buckwheat per pound..........................	05

Honey Extractors furnished at manufacturers' prices, the best in the market.

Address:

J. M. HICKS & CO.,
Battle Ground,
Tippecanoe County, Ind.

N. B.—Always be particular to write your name and address plainly, to avoid mistakes.

☞ I desire to procure good energetic Agents throughout the United States and Territories, to whom liberal commissions will be allowed, as well as good premiums in Bees, Italian Queens, and Hicks Hives, including the *North American Bee-Keepers' Guide*, a book up with the times in Bee-keeping, which retails at fifty cents per single copy, and is worth ten times the price to any farmer or person contemplating going into the Bee business.

Address, with inclosed stamp for terms, and you will always hear from me. *J. M. HICKS.*

I also wish to negotiate and make arrangements for all first-class honey, for which I will pay cash or exchange Italian Queens, or Hicks Bee Hives, with or without bees in the same. In a word, I will exchange any article I keep for sale to supply Bee-keepers with for good, first-class honey, at fair prices.

J. M. HICKS,
Battle Ground,
Tippecanoe County, Ind.

J. M. HICKS & CO.

WILL FURNISH

TRIMMINGS AND HARDWARE

—FOR—

Hicks' Bee Hives,

—ALSO—

A Full Set of Transferring Tools,

FOR AGENTS, FURNISHED ON SHORT NOTICE,

We are also prepared to furnish the best

Honey-Extractors,

AT MANUFACTURERS' PRICES.

Knives for Uncapping Honey,

and WAX-EXTRACTORS,

Will also be furnished on Short Notice and at Low Price

Address all orders to

J. M. HICKS & CO.,
Battle Ground,
Tippecanoe County, Ind.

☞ The Best and Purest Stock of Brama Chickens furnished on reasonable terms for cash. It is a well-known fact that the two families of Bramas—that of dark and light—if bred together, make the most hardy and best chickens for the market, and by far the richest, sweetest and best meat for use.

Address all orders to **J. M. HICKS & CO.,**
Battle Ground, Ind.

 **Price 50c., Postpaid.**

THE
NORTH AMERICAN
Bee - Keepers'
GUIDE,

BY J. M. HICKS,
Practical Apiarian,
Battle Ground, Tippecanoe Co., Ind.

LAFAYETTE
BEE STEAM PRINTING HOUSE,
 J. L. COX & BRO., PRINTERS.
1875.

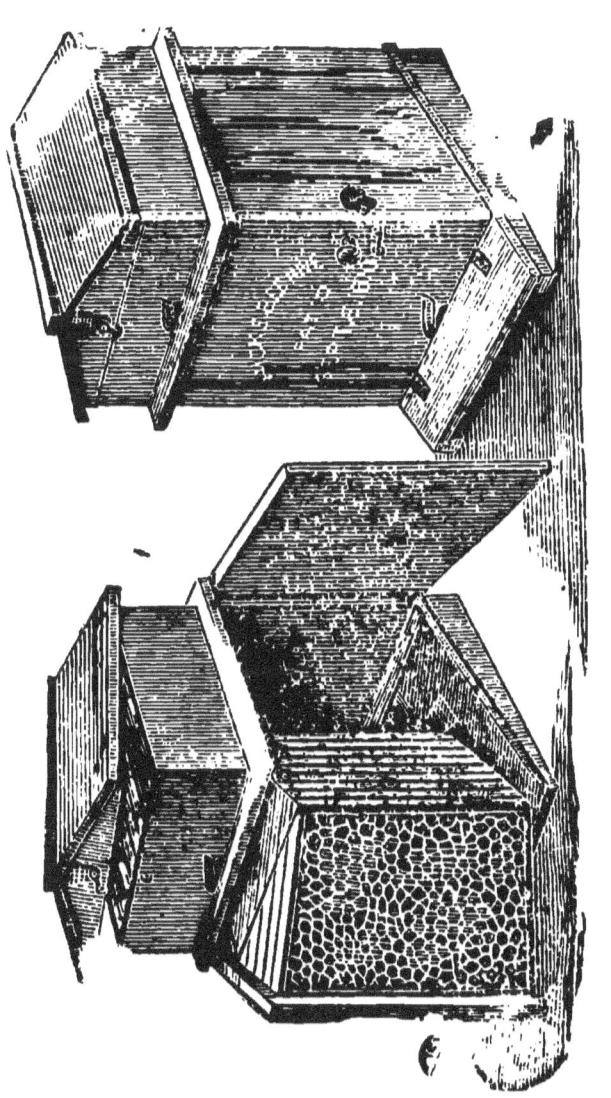

Hicks' Competition Bee-Hive

www.ingramcontent.com/pod-product-compliance
Lightning Source LLC
Chambersburg PA
CBHW030903170426
43193CB00009BA/726